Tate

I recognized a brother -
a comrade on the journey
in you - I look forward
to finding a trail together

John

i

Reading Jeff Hood's brilliant first collection of poems we get to experience how one man lives his soul path. His I–Thou relationship with everything includes scrambling up rocky ridges, writing poems, flowing through white water, and nurturing his blessed apricot tree. This modern-day Thoreau invites us in to the struggle to make his livelihood support his quest, to make sense of the consumptive culture we've created, and especially to explore his relationship with the mysterious divine feminine.

Men who want to live your hero's journey, and women who want to support your man's quest, here is a guide book calling us to be the pine in the wind, to fly through the snow, to know the sacred in your lover's touch, even to find music in the sound of traffic.

Jane Lipman, Poet, *On the Back Porch of the Moon*,
Winner of the 2013 New Mexico/Arizona Book Award
and a NM Press Women's Award

Musk Ox Poems, by Jeff Hood, is a celebration of worms, an apology to an owl, a love note to an apricot tree. It is a "dance between the dirty dishes and the dessert" that incorporates the gritty and difficult along with the sweet and easy. He honors the scrape of the trowel "describing the arc of the moon" and the sweat of splitting wood in autumn to earn winter's warmth. The poems express love of Mother Earth, who puts "cranberries on the table, fleece jackets on our backs" and a moral urgency to take care of her creatures. In Hood's poems, a snapping turtle is "forty pounds/of ancient slow-moving wisdom" and a bullsnake found in the house is addressed as "sweetheart." These are poems of a man who is comfortable in his body, as it "carves a turn at high speed through snow" and as it aches with aging and the labor that he relishes. It is a book of honoring and joy, a work that doesn't hesitate to take the reader down to "the inevitable dark goo," nor holds back from speaking the bliss of arriving at places above timberline where "everything yearns for up."

Donald Levering, Winner of the Tor House Foundation Robinson Jeffers Prize and author of *Coltrane's God, Previous Lives,* and *Any Song Will Do.*

Musk Ox Poems

Jeff Hood

Musk Ox Poems

Some poems have been published previously,
some in other versions.

The author thanks the following journals:
Canyon Voices, Arizona State University On-line
Literary Magazine
Wingspan Journal of the Male Spirit
The Story Mandala, Center for Renewal and
Wholeness in Higher Education

ISBN: 9781071448687
Imprint: Independently published

CONTENTS

DEDICATION

ACKNOWLEDGEMENTS

INTRODUCTION

HER MAJESTY

A Celebration of Worms 2
Owl 3
A Love Note 4
The Cascade 5
Earth Lover 6
Your Invitation 7
Forest Friends 8
Straight Out of a Dream 9
I Am Not the God 11
My Clock 12
Singing 13
Almost 14
Bananas 15
Earth Mother 16
How Would I Know 18
Eden 19
Spring's Chaos 21
Neighbors 22
Skier's Lover 23
Eden II 24
Blue 25
Pomegranate 26

MEN'S STUFF

Old Man's Hands 28
HELP! 29
Warrior 31
Jack Orion 32
Just a Haircut 33
Guardian Angel 35

Elemental Introductions 37
What If? 39
Snapping Turtle 40
Encounter 41
The Price of Your Soul 43

WILD

Into a Glory 46
"Original Blessing" 47
Wet Socks 48
Blue Gate 49
Perspective 50
Elephant Heads 52
A Practice 53
Sitting 54
September 27 55
Stuck in a Tree Well 56
Works Get in the Way 57
Sitting on Ice 58
The Best Therapy I
Know 59
Thumbing 61
A Radical Thing
Down 63
Tiger Stripes 64
A Swim 68
Caught Napping 69
"When I Met My Muse" 70
The Wild Animal of My
Soul 72

PEOPLE POLITIC

The Week Before Christmas
2004   74
Sympathy for the Devil   77
Ali   78
Un Apologia   79
A Teacher's Plea   80
Easter Immigrant   82
What If?   83

REFLECTIONS

A Message   86
Ever   87
The Miracle of Now   88
Broken Glass   89

Can I Stop?   90
Dad's '49 Flatbed   91
Claiming My Name   92
Strangers?   93
Life at Four Miles an
Hour   95
Resolution Bay   96
Tilt   97
Aging's Paradox   98
Grief   100
Kodi's End   101
Proof of God?   102
Ode to Jake Sully   103
Self   104
Amy   105
Caroline   106
Ripley   107
Wounds   108
Alone   109
What If Forgiveness?   110

No small thing,
To sing the name of God
Enough to believe it

DEDICATION

I dedicate this book to Mother Earth and the abundance of the garden. Along with my dog, Lili, you are the source of unconditional love. To all the women I've mistaken for the Goddess, forgive me, I get confused when I'm hungry. To all the good men in my life, thank God for comrades on the journey.

And to Musk Ox. I spent a month in the Arctic a while back; and, of all the wonders, I most wanted to see these most resilient, gentle, communal monsters. And how can you resist their name?

ACKNOWLEDGEMENTS

I want to acknowledge: The Celebration community, for listening so enthusiastically over the years. My every other Sunday evening poetry circle, for including the breaking of bread together with our passion for the spoken word. My friend Rebekah Mathiesen for offering her print of a Musk Ox. And all the other good friends who have asked for more. I look forward to the opportunity to read them aloud.

I especially want to acknowledge my brother Bruce, who played the ogre when we were young. And my sister Penny for whom I played it as well. Thank God we don't have to do that anymore. And my best friend Rose. May we continue to learn to love.

INTRODUCTION

I might have been six years old when I heard a favorite aunt refer to me as a "sensitive boy." Looking back, she was accurate. I recall asking my mom to teach me to cook and sew. My best friend, Suzie Lister, lived down the street. And I didn't take to baseball. This was the kiss of death with my older brother and his friends. I suffered at their hands and words. And when I got to junior high school in the sixties, I also discovered that the term "sensitive boy" was associated with the few unfortunate effeminate losers, the "queers" in school. I felt terribly sorry for them, more than a little alarmed at my attraction to their access to feelings, and pretty sure I didn't want to run that gauntlet. Managing to drum up some red-blooded American masculinity, I joined the football team, found a buddy to go fishing with, grew an appreciation for splintered and calloused hands, and discovered a passion for flying down mountains in the snow, all acceptably masculine pursuits.

I've managed to dance a life between the sensitive boy who still mends his gear on a sewing machine, loves to cook, and writes poetry; and the guy who enjoys watching football, drinking beer and farting, in reverse order.

I share all this as an introduction to a maturing relationship with the capital "F" Feminine, who won't be squeezed into paragraphs following the rules of grammar and punctuation. She comes to me in dreams and through my intimate relationship with our planet, our Mother Earth. My first encounter was of course through my own mother, an impossible and conflicted comparison with the Divine. Then mistakenly pursued with more lovers than I'm proud to admit. I have regularly made the terrible mistake of comparing you to Her. I apologize. It's just that you look so much like Her, and you have this wonderful ability to offer yourself in the most delicious and sacred ways. An excruciating mystery for sure.

This Divine Feminine wants to be known, yet Her mystery will not be revealed through microscopes or scientific journals with references to obscure experiments in Baltimore.

To say that I've chosen to explore Her presence is like saying I choose to pump my heart. She is here, feeding, clothing and sheltering, giving and taking life in Her time, and I've been blessed to witness the miracle. She comes and goes as She pleases. In dreams She's a meadow daisy, a tripped-out rock and roll star from the '70s, and a blue white light high in a spruce tree on the coast of Maine. In waking life, my most reliable encounters take place in wild places where I regularly go to escape the hustle; where She reliably reminds me that mortgages, taxes, traffic and deadlines are just dust blowing in our human wind, while Her vital calendar follows the pulse of the tide, of snow-melt rivers in spring, and the clockwork spin of our planet through inky cold space. Here is where I experience unconditional love.

To imagine that a destructive hurricane growing out of Her rising temperature is an expression of anger or vengeance completely misses the mark, for She is incapable of that too-human quality of vicious payback. Wilhelm Reich once asked, *Did you ever stop to think how much the earth gives, without ever asking anything in return?* The increasing ferocity of our hurricanes, tornadoes and draughts, is nothing more than a natural consequence of our ignorance and industry. Our lesson is to discover how to live in harmony and gratitude.

In all humility, I don't think I could have opened to the Feminine mystery had I not been so blessed with this magnificent masculine body that pushing seventy years, still loves the roar of rapids, skiing faster than is prudent, and swinging an axe, or shovel, or hammer; and the accompanying brotherhood of men who share it. I am doubly blessed with a circle of men willing to explore the roots of our power through our vulnerability. There is no mystery here, but a celebration and a vast appreciation for a fraternity of healthy questing.

Time to let the poems speak. I've separated them in categories, but please flip back and forth. They don't like to be put in boxes.

Her Majesty

A Celebration of Worms

I spread the summer compost today,
then turned the garden over shovel by shovel.
Red wigglers galore.
They corkscrew in fear
the instant they feel light and air.
But I imagine them diving back down
to pursue the rot of purpled banana peel,
crushed eggshell and old zucchini.

How different from us topsiders
who scramble in avoidance
of the inevitable dark goo
of being put underground.

I roust them out,
then try to cover them,
hoping they'll be there
when I make my descent.
My friends of the underworld.

Owl

Would I give up driving
to save your life, Owl?
Or your brother's life
as it were?

Could I learn how
to compost and mulch
to keep from chopping
my friend worm in half?

I've begun to consider
not slapping the little fruit flies
that share my home.
What harm?

But quit driving?!
On the probability that
some country road and I
will conspire to snatch
the life of a creature
whose velvet wings hinge out
in a striped fan of silence,
and whose toes underneath
those scimitars could be
my four-fingered hand?

Bless you, Owl.
I am so terribly sorry
that we have learned
to fly faster than you.

A Love Note

I just want you to know. . .

has it been 10 years
since I've moved in with you?!

The velvet golden curve
of your breasts in July,
taste of your birth opening
dark seed revealing,
aroma on the breeze
upon waking early morning. . .

Your fortitude through storm and drought,
tolerance of my neglect,
and your striving to feed me
with all you have . . .

that it's fine with me
my friend, blessed apricot,
if you take a rest this year
because your exquisite pink petals
opening to this imperfect world
succumb to a late March frost.

The Cascade

I thought I knew Her skirts.
Intimate with meadow grasses swishing
back and forth in waves,
rush of wind through an aspen canopy,
approach of rustling leaves one side,
dancing away on the other.

Yesterday as I came to the cascade,
a tumble of silver spray
calling out to the sun,
She introduced herself anew.
Misty curtains whirling, curling out and up,
She flung them left and right
far out in my face,
pure delight.
To come back, a rush and roar
over Her mound of mossy black basalt.

Waking now, still full of our encounter,
I trust She never slept a minute.
Unconcerned with conservation,
She's there still, dancing
as dawn peeks over the ridge.
Singing Her abundance of living,
laughing water
to the eager earth below.

Earth Lover

If you do not have a regular practice
of embracing your Mother,
I mean getting out in a whipping storm
to roll around in the snow,
sticking your nose in the bark of a pine tree
to discover Her scent,
finding the right dish of needles
in which to make your bed,
dropping whatever the fuck
seems so important, to walk down the street
to the patch of dirt that is unclaimed
and unkempt by human interference,
to find Her living presence
and drop down on your knees
to kiss Her folded flesh
and say "I love you!"
Then . . .

What?

What meltdown of all our industry would I avenge?
What dark crackling lightning bolt would I call in Her
defense?
What crashing seas and tumbling mountains
should rain down on us ungrateful ants
who have the sight but refuse to see?

While She, in Her blessing,
will continue to put cranberries on the table,
fleece jackets on our backs,
celebrate our births and bleed in our wars

                    alone.

Your Invitation

Yesterday You called me.
Your sentinels, the pines,
waving their arms,
in love with the wind.

In that ecstasy I knew
I couldn't climb You safely.

Assuming the invitation is open,
I've chosen this morning
to make the ascent,
to taste Your nectar.

And decided it's better
not to act one's age.
That rule was made
for fuddy-duddies
afraid to remember
what it feels like to hug
the top of a tree in the wind.

Forest Friends

On the radio the other day,
a German forester
described how trees communicate.
When caterpillars attack,
leaves change their scent,
roots send messages
through the network of mycelia
so their neighbors can prepare.
But the signals travel at the speed of trees.

Sometimes, when I've escaped the sound of traffic,
quit crashing from one thing to the next,
I imagine I hear them, in deep-throated, green voices.
Slow voices.

It gives me reason to tread softly on their toes,
perspective on what a bulldozer can do
to scrape bare rock on this forest road,
not to mention concrete and asphalt.
Can they possibly sing their songs
under such darkness?

Straight Out of a Dream

She's coming
as inevitably as summer
in all her glory, more than abundance,
the chaos of green, running
down the paths, up
in the trees, meadows.
Heralded by robins, black birds, larks,
sweetest little canyon wren
down in the shadows.
She's coming.

The word is out, all along the coast.
Clear the decks!
Roll out a living carpet.
Meadow daisies float out to meet her.

True, the water is a mess, our refuse
everywhere, we've soiled our source.

Those who have heard, crowd the shore,
leap into boats, children, careless,
splash in the filth.

She's coming and we don't even know
what to expect, her name, or
what she looks like.
We're scared.

Microphones in pieces,
loose wires, no batteries,
parts arrive, cobbled together.
The pianist is here, show tunes galore,
but I don't know her song,
and I'm scared.

From backstage a talisman appears,
rough character standing guard
at the meadow gate.

She's coming, like a flower,
fierce, delicate, patient,
earth mover, water spirit.
All I have is my song.
All I have is my song.

I Am Not the God

I am not the God
tho I am happy to represent Him to you
in power and passion
to fill you with my love.

I know that you are not the Goddess
tho your representation
is entirely satisfying.

I find Her in your eyes, your smile
and when I enter you,

She fills me with tears.

My Clock

A day is not made up
of hours and minutes
waiting for cocktails at five.
It is the growing red face of the cliff at sunrise,
shade creeping along this rock at noon,
caterpillar lumping along,
head in every crevice
—for the food that will
allow him a butterfly—
completely unconcerned with
the schedule of flights
to Los Angeles.

Singing

Waves thundered and crashed
or lapped ever so softly
on the beach
at night
singing me to sleep
as a child.

The song changed
depending on Her temperament.
But, as with the eternal tide,
She never stopped singing.

A few times I have let another's life
become that constant.

A song, coming in
and going out,
now fierce,
now laughing,
now gently lapping
on my beach.

Breathing faster than She does,
this human endurance illusory.
The song that has lit my life
moves on.

Is it a mistake?
Should I attach
to God, a Guru, the Tide,
to avoid the loss?

Or take up singing?

Almost

When I wake
to the sound of traffic,
I can almost turn it into
the rush of waves on a beach
far from my bedroom window.

The length of plastic hose
looping from the stream bank
could be a smooth root reaching out
and back again in search of life.
And the rapid formed around
an old truck body appears somewhat
like it belongs, if I don't look too closely.

But the hotel on the hill
attempting to light up the night
cannot possibly be mistaken for
moonrise, and the hollow beneath my heart
is the price I pay for such fantasies.

The tax collector has already been to my door
and I found it easier to write the check
than stand and argue.

But what about the distant call of waves?

Bananas

The first thing you have noticed
is the offering,
slim white penis
peeled out of his yellow jacket
delicate and oh-so-sweet when ripe,
not so incongruous for a fruit.

But, my God!
the flower from which they emerge,
blazing in bunches,
huge purple torpedo,
wanting to devour us all.

Earth Mother

Earth Mother, anima,
fuentes, Spring of life,
soul, Parvati, Membraiute.*
You are the one, the breast
from which we all drink.

I fall on my face at Your feet
my tears are inadequate
and too salty,
but they are all I have to give.

Not so. You will take my blood,
my semen, and the
water of my cells.

And what of my prayers and passion?
Do they serve You at all?
At the least they wake me up
so that I may tread
a little more lightly
over Your precious flesh.

Mother of all
forgive me for wearing muddy boots
in Your house.

Too often do I
turn on the tap
or flip the switch
without thanking You,
giving no thought to my waste.

I find mylar balloons stuck
in the forest of Your lungs.
Rubber tires and worse
collect in cholesterol dams in Your streams,

16

yet we will all be surprised
when Your heart stops ticking.

The cancer grows
and You keep smiling,
yet Your milk is less sweet,
and I see the strain in concrete
smudges under Your eyes.

My garden is barren,
no rain falls.
At 20 till midnight
I rush around thinking
something is to be done.

I pray for forgiveness
without deserving
and Raven, laughing,
drops a branch on my head.

*Balinese Earth Goddess

How Would I know

that the sound of traffic,
like rust in the hull,
was eating my integrity,
unless I'd lived
with water and wave
and wind in the pines?

———————

Sorry to disturb your fishing,
little heron.
And since I'm not here to eat,
away I go.

Eden

Some of you will attach more importance
to which of them picked the apple from the tree.
Eve-the temptress, the seeker, the curious;
or Adam-the stolid, the obedient, the victim.
I do to the extent that they both play
on the see-saw of my being.

In any case, we ate. And it was good.
And our eyes opened to knowledge;
curiously, first to our nakedness,
then shame, fear and separation.

One would think we'd first look up
at the wondrous world, the shine of the apple,
glint of light in Eve's hair, robin singing,
checkered snake sliding ever so gracefully.

Had we been Buddhists, we might have.

But no, our knowledge separated us from all that.
Desire for comfort and commodity
prompted us to clothe ourselves.
Then to till the earth, sweat,
bear children in pain,
build hospitals, bridges, schools,
develop scientific explanations for the wonders
we'd simply lived just a short time before.

Never thinking that our roofs, books and factories,
though increasing our comfort,
shut out the seed sprouting spring-green leaf
pushing up through earth's brown skin,
shield us from moon's silver face
so big rising over the mountain;
somehow convince us we are apart
even from our beloved dogs who streak
here and there in pursuit of smells beyond.

It's not the morals of the game that concern me,
our increasingly important political rights and wrongs,
but the results we reap; the bulldozers in the forest
and miles of plastic covering the ocean.
No blame to Eve, that curious aspect of our nature.
Self-forgiveness to Adam, for passing the buck.

It's time to take responsibility for the wonders of our garden,
find comfort in the inevitability of pain, in birth and death.
We have a short time to do so
before we are truly cast out of the garden.

Spring's Chaos

What will no doubt
soon become a tailored lawn
in Spring's chaos
is a litter of dead leaves.
Winter's twigs,
piles of worm castings, and
exuberant green things emerging
out of place.

The gardener is occupied elsewhere
and Earth is busy expressing herself.

Neighbors

Bullsnake blessed me today.
My head in the pantry, shopping for supper,
when she poked out under the door.
Always a shock, followed by delight.
I've had a couple visits since the cat left.
Dressed in her large weave tweeds,
curious, shy, respectful,
she retreated to a corner.
Pretty sure neither of us wanted her inside anymore.
But how to get her out without trauma,
to make sure she assumed welcome tomorrow.
My quick grab behind her head
and she twisted around my arm
in fear for her life no doubt.
No, no, sweetheart. You belong here.
Out to the rock wall
where I've seen mice
who think they're safe.

Skier's Lover

Unbroken breast of gleaming snow falls below
running out in aspen gold.
Twenty, maybe thirty turns beckon.
Who can count such beauty?
And yet we stand, just tasting.

She knows about foreplay,
this lover of a billion years,
who lies waiting, calling,
eager for our ecstasy.

Our question, "Who goes first?"
is too small. She calls us all.

We write our bliss in wavy lines upon Her flesh.
Growls and screams echo forward
to where I sit at my desk,
still panting.

Eden II

The scientists are finally discovering
that we've been given a gift.
Something sparked two hundred thousand years ago,
a chromosome tweaked here,
a gene missing over there.

And we started asking, "Please pass the salt,"
adjusted our hair as we looked into still pools,
solved puzzles, sought comfort, avoided pain.

Adam had something to say about it,
blistered hands, all Eve's fault,
yet so easy to feel special, chosen, separate.

His assumption
that we are no longer beholden,
our deserving of dominance
the true cross we bear.

Beavers, after all, have yet to discover cement,
canyon wren has no designs on a Grammy,
and faithful doggo is incapable of a vengeful thought.

On a hike along the piney coast of Maine one time,
we came upon a skeletal hand,
complete with its complex wrist leading to radius and ulna.
Yet the five-digited fingers were a foot-and-a-half long,
 wrist bones stretched to alien proportion.

A little research revealed it to have been a seal flipper
no doubt dragged up by a coyote and left to shed its skin.

A reminder that we are all
still children of Eden.

Blue

I've been trying to describe
New Mexico sky blue for forty years.
It is beyond language,
the difference between reading
and hearing "Amazing Grace."
An exultation of blue!

Just now I've woken from a nap
back stiff and cold from the meadow.
Three hours into a ramble
up and down from twelve thousand feet.
Rush of living water tumbling,
pumping over rocks,
sometime gusts of breath through spruce,
fierce sun up here mid-October,
flaming aspens reaching up
so close to God,
wrapped in Her skirts.

Doggo wears it well,
more familiar, singing Her song, in tune.
I envy her, folded into this living music,
yet knowing it not.

Perhaps in sleep I wore the cloak
of belonging, this blue cloak,
and now recall the notes
just after sleeping Her song.

Pomegranate

The qualities of the pomegranate include
the time it takes to split the skin
to reveal the bounty of rubies
packed and wrapped ever so carefully
in their egg cartons of waxed paper.
In order to honor them properly one must,
with increasingly sticky red fingers,
seek out each jewel in its hiding place,
amassing shining little nuggets
while the anticipation of
explosions on the tongue mounts.

A twisted French military connoisseur
gave their name to his grenade.
Pharaohs in Egypt were buried with them.
Jesus could have been weaned to their juice.
And we moderns are so busy
we prefer to buy our red gems
sorted by others' hands
and vacuum packed in plastic,
missing the experience entirely.

MEN'S STUFF

Old Man's Hands

Old man flying alone.
Your hands give you away,
flesh grown round your wedding ring
like a tree flowing around a cable
wrapped and abandoned years ago.

Left index finger lost who knows when
as a young man worked carelessly.
In counterpoint,
the forefinger on your right
sports a creased nail,
smashed once and forever telling the tale.

Now shaking, paper-skinned,
blue plumbing shows
where muscle once lived.
Scabs that appear out of nowhere.

Those are eighty-year hands
if I've ever seen them.

Landing in Atlanta to transfer,
I can't help but find mine,
piled strong and healthy,
well used yet ringless on the seat back.
Wondering what story they may tell
thirty years hence.

Of a sudden loneliness I sit,
"Can I give you a hand
with anything?"

A younger man's smile,
"No thank you, I'm going on to D.C.
Have a happy Thanksgiving."

And a younger man's spirit reached
through that old claw to shake mine
as the blessing flowed both ways.

HELP!

I'm the healthiest man I know.
My cholesterol, antioxidants and prostate are fine.
My bare feet know the feel
of pine needles,
and my eyes can see
the horizon from atop near hills.

I know the difference between
excitement and fear.
And sometimes I find the courage
to catch myself
in the middle of making
you wrong.

Yet
I don't know my brother.
You won't talk to me
about our childhood.
So I can't tell
what is real.

When my dreams
are violent
and my gun won't shoot
to kill the men who chase me,
I can't find North
on the compass
and my dog, great as he is
can only console me
so far.

Help!
The veil
that separates me
from the one who would
bonk you on the head
and take your woman

grows thin.
And I am afraid.

Help.
I am also afraid that we will
continue to be nice to each other.
That the armor around my chest
will grow,
not crack.
That I will continue
to cry alone
without you,
my brother,
to put my head
on your breast.

If I must do this alone,
or find a woman to listen,
I'll go mad,
and the gorilla will stay
in his cage.

We may not need
to say it all,
but I have a great desire
to push on you
and have you push back.
To sweat and struggle together.
To look fear
in his face
and know you are
Here.

I have a great desire
for the laughter
that comes after.
I'm not sure
I can find it
without you.

Warrior

I walked into a dark room
carrying
my luggage.

You took it all away.
"You don't need all this crap!"

I surprised myself:
"You're right,
Thank God!"

Jack Orion

You introduced yourself
through my November bedroom window
when I was six.
You listened with celestial calm
to my nocturnal terrors.

Through the sarcasm of an older brother
I was instructed
that I had you upside down.
That my joyful dancer
was in fact a warrior.
Sword and shield
facing his opponent, Taurus.

I still get up at four a.m. mid-August
to welcome your night-by-night swing
across the coming winter sky.

Standing centuries
of masculine attraction
to violence on its head,
I greet you dancing.
A jig perhaps.
And faithful Sirius
turning a flip.

Just a Haircut

Tuesday, I got a haircut.
No sooner in the door
than a four-year-old, big-eyed boy
announces to me that his arm hurts.
"I'm sorry. What happened?"

"Can I help you?"
Name on the list,
I sit with a magazine.

Here he is again.
"What's in your pocket?"

OK, cutie.
Your mom cuts hair.
This waiting room is your preschool.
Men are scarce in your life.
Your inquisitiveness has explored
women's things, no doubt.

But what does a man carry?
What masculine magic
lurks in that khaki pouch?

He draws me out.
Or is it in?
Recalling my innocence
fifty years ago.

My pride,
his vulnerability,
exposes the talisman:
my Swiss Army Knife.

As if the crown jewels
have been revealed,
he sighs, squirming

onto the bench.

First the corkscrew,
mysterious pigtail,
is traced and explained
in sign and simple imagery.

We go primal.
Leaving time,
we are in a firelit hut,
smoke and leather, knapping flint.

Then blades and can opener
and back to the corkscrew.
In his hand now.
He knows to stay away from sharps.
I help open the others.

Toothpick and tweezers
occupy us for hours
when they call my name.

"Who does that bright little boy
belong to?
We've just spent the last ten minutes
exploring the contents of my pocket."

Her look of alarm
brings me back to the twenty-first century,
where it might not be safe
for a strange man
to show a young boy
anything in his pocket,
not even a jackknife.

Guardian Angel

I've felt his hand on my back
since I can remember.

Our first encounter, in the dark of night,
he emerged from the closet,
robed and bald but for a topknot.
I woke screaming.

Later, I'd pick him up when I passed the Tulu tree
on the way to the beach.
He must have known
I was running from family demons.

He was with me throwing rocks at bottles,
explosions of freedom in the water.

Through a boy's rough and tumble,
teen dancing with danger,
young adult in a chemical haze,
he was there, pulling me up and out.

A deferment from the draft.
Introductions to excitable women,
kind men, white forests, muddy rivers.
Urging me out to the garden,
the miracle of green and blue.

Here on the other side of life's bell curve,
I'm blessed to embody this magnificent temple,
and know it as I've come to know him.

He pops his head up as I lose a job
three months before retirement,
helping me patch together bits and pieces to keep it going.

You'd think I'd have learned to trust by now,
to do my part in crafting outcomes.
And perhaps I have,
for the bus keeps trundling down the road.
His Merlin to my Arthur.
The lesson gleaned, both dark and light,
giving me reason to laugh, be kind, pass it on.

Elemental Introductions

I am the oak tree
for you to crash into,
fists, words, tears.
After a while you will
lie down in my deep leaves
with your head on my roots,
or climb to the sky
in my rough and brown arms,

or walk away.

I am the steel gray ocean
and you may sail upon me
fishing your dinner.
But keep an eye to the weather
for I may take you down.

I am the little camp fire
of twigs and pine cones
come to warm your hands
in the middle of a cold and hungry night,
huddled then nursed until
no charcoal remains to tell the tale
to a forest full of twigs.

I am the breeze before dawn
up under the coat of your dark night.
You may jump and shiver
hoping you see light
but you're not sure
until I come again later
with the scent of coffee and cinnamon.

And you could walk away.
But where would you go?

You are the young boy on my beach

courting waves, throwing rocks at bottles.
With pop and whoop they break
sinking to where I roll them
over and over in time
delivering you sanded gems
of green, brown and blue.

I am the spray of apple
first bite, that you never knew
could taste in the roof of your mouth.

You look out from a photograph of an innocent
twelve-year-old, wondering at the world.
I hold the frame, the wall, the window.
I am the light upon your face.

I waited in branches, just above your head
should you have looked up through the tears
on your way to the beach to throw rocks.

I wait here still.

What If?

What if all we are here for
is to learn to be kind?

What if kneeling down
eye to eye with a crying child,
or carrying the spider outside
instead of squashing it,
or holding back on the caustic comment
to a friend who has taken more than she gives
because she grew up in a house full of trolls . . .

What if?

And I've spent all these years
practicing karate with my words, and
digging up the graveyard of my life, and
bobbing for sour green apples
plastered with dollar signs, and
pretending to be nice,
and, and, and, and, and . . .

What if I can finally
not have to hold my shoulders up
like a man?

Snapping Turtle

Attractive just because
you were the biggest predator
in our young world.

Forty pounds
of ancient slow-moving wisdom,
a golden star in each eye
and beak to stay clear of.

We pursued you, prehistoric hunter,
from out of the mud, for years.
And when finally captured,
you sported the scars of battle.
Your inglorious death taught us all something
about senseless killing.

Encounter

They'd been shucking and jiving all day.
The push and shove, verbal battle that passes
for counting coup in today's desperate young men
jockeying for position while avoiding work.

By the end of the day, I'd had enough,
when a condom fell out of a pocket
and they were off and running about the size,
color and qualities.

I said, "STOP! This conversation is not appropriate for a classroom
and it's not appropriate out here."

"I can talk any fucking way I want!"

I lost it. "You're out of here! Get out!"

"What are you going to do, call the cops?"

It got worse.
I'm sure my voice rose,
fists clenched, inches from getting down
in the dirt with this young man.

He had me, but he'd lost himself.
It's what they do, push until someone goes over the edge
and violence hangs in the moment
as all go tumbling over Niagara,
testosterone surging through veins
in a rush we've all sought.

I stepped back, the group was silent for eternity,
when my partner stepped in.
They don't mess with Leroy.
They left. It was over.

Except for the 240 volts pumping up and down my body.

I was up in the middle of the night, and next day,
couldn't shake it.

Something primal, soulful, demanding.
I thought I'd been dancing with that wildness all my life,
a relationship I've cultivated in whitewater and on mountain tops,
but this was different, darker, out of control.
Can you breathe through this to find his humanity?
And your own?

Adults have been kicking him out of classrooms all his life.
I'll not join that club, been there, on both sides.
Redemption possible for both of us in the power of vulnerability.
And god bless him, he showed up the next week.

The Price of Your Soul

"Huu-uuggghh!"
whiskered growl
rises out of leaf mold

to brush away
my smoky attempts
at meaning.

No electric cup of tea
in that fist.

The gaps in his teeth
show dark and deep,
familiar of seaweed
and fat white grubs.

"Lost in the woods?!
HAH!"

One rooty finger
calls forth the North wind.

"Attend me, you fool!
I own you now!
Your precious keys
and bank accounts
are dirt under my nails.

You can hear my heart
beat in your chest
and your terror is deserved
for I have your balls in my claw.

Get out in the night
with your father's shrunken hands
to gather boughs for my bed.

You'll not sleep tonight.
And the price of your soul
I'll know in the morning."

WILD

Into a Glory

I ski down
out of the sun.

Nuclear core
reflected in cloud
beckons me to
where sky and snow
become one.

Flying, through the aurora.
Exploding, bounded only
by how many diamonds
I can breathe
to keep my legs from
burning up.

Folded in the mist
too wild now to slow
to a sensible descent.

Take me, glory.
This Earth-bound life
needs you.

Original Blessing
      Thanks to Matthew Fox

On a day such as this
first man looked up from
his morning's labor of hafting a spear
at the wind blowing spruce and a hint of smoke
and the blue green
reflection of sky on the bay
that only yesterday was grey.

And realized he was one,
that the breeze was for him
and the gull,
that his mossy pillow
had its own life in the sun,
that the joint of his finger
matched grasshopper's knee,
and Eve's apple
was as sweet as she.

Wet Socks

Kids in the woods, lots of them.
There will be more noise than a city street.
They will leave plastic wrappers
hidden in places only the squirrels can find.
Some of them won't want to pee in the bushes,
so hold it, which will dominate their experience.
And when they've gone screeching back to the bus,
green growing things will be left trampled
and unsung among the chaos of footprints.

But some of them will look up through the pine boughs
at the blue sky and wonder what clouds are made of
and find themselves drinking green into their souls.
Others, in ecstasy, will get soaked in the creek
while identifying benthic macroinvertebrates.
And maybe one or two, fifteen years from now,
will find herself studying ecology in grad school,
or writing poetry about mayfly larvae wrapped in their wet socks.

Blue Gate

My friend's clipped and cared-for backyard
falls down progressively more wild
to a fence in which a blue gate opens.
A portal through which
a dark riot unkempt
calls me deep to where
water snake hunts fish
and raccoon hunts him.

They all fear me
no less than I fear myself,
Adam cast out,
forever looking back,
engaged in the contest
between tinkling rapid,
bird call, seed fall,
and erratic rush of auto over bridge.

Come with me now!
Red bird calls
from high in his tree.
And I've seen his mate
sneak into the thicket.

Perspective

In order to see Polaris trace a tiny circle
up there in his impossibly distant and frigid space
you must first lie out all night
without the intention
of getting the best night's sleep.

Next, your bed has to position you
so the star can be found winking
at his cousins in the great bear
who are so obviously rounding the night sky.
Dipping below our North
and emerging in the East pre-dawn.

But most importantly, you need perspective,
an intermediate point, seemingly stable,
firmly attached to our lovely spinning planet.

Mine was the finger rock
of a canyon rim a mile away
round which my quarry danced
as I woke in the wind,
checked incoming puffs of cloud,
got up to pee, or pulled covers over.

Discovering that sleep was inconsequential
compared to the miracle whirling overhead.

Elephant Heads

And why, he asked,
is that your favorite flower
in the whole world?

Because it has about twenty
pink little trunks
and each trunk
has a pair of floppy pink ears

and it only grows up here
where there is a 10,000 volt definition
between ridge and heaven,

where you can nap on spongy sod
but a smooth rock will do as well,

where the test of a weary-kneed descent,
to make sure we are still alive,
is to launch naked into the lake
still birthing in snow fields
and come out confirmed,

where those little elephants
celebrate every rise and drop
in the precious arc of the sun.

A Practice

Neurosis is always a substitute for legitimate suffering
- Carl Jung

I ponder Jung's statement
while climbing a big hill.

No hurry, step, breathe, step,
over that root, up a little rock ramp,
huff, feeling it now.

Forsake the worn trail
for this elegant granite ridge,
careful, considered, in a way
that life down below too easily avoids.

Somewhere in the dance,
the breath comes into me,

Focus on this finger nub.
Can I step up on that point?

a joy, a presence, union, pacing,
fire in my legs, wind in my sails,
and this magnificent pile of rock.

Legitimate suffering? Absolutely!
Like grief, loneliness, fear?
Is this unavoidable for those waking,
walking in this world?

This torment of climbing,
I choose.
A practice, leaving scant room for doubt, stalling,
all my usual tactics.
While God whispers, "higher, higher!"

Sitting

I've been sitting,
just sitting
in the sun.

Treasuring less
the business to be done
than the riot
of bougainvillea in the window
and the conversation of little birds.

I'll get up soon
and be productive.
But I've discovered
it's a flicker who has been
digging ant larvae
from between the flagstones,
and the taste of green things
in the air sustains me.

September 27

First snow on the mountain
and every step outside
takes my gaze up there,
where the old man's breath
turns to crystal in his beard.
I want to join him
huffing and puffing up his shoulder
to where only Raven
can climb some more.
There to stop earning my joy,
loose this firm connection,
spread my wings
and fly.

Stuck in a Tree Well

Flinging himself about in the snow,
spread-eagled, face down,
no room to breathe,
nothing to push up on,
skis a tangle up above.
Having launched an undetermined distance
through blue sparkling stratosphere
because there were just too many arcs
carved in acceleration
on her glistening parchment.
He finds the breath, the joy,
the explosive relief to laugh.

Words Get in The Way

High on a rock face,
wind crafting unwanted chaos
between my collar and ear.
Your yells a jumble
of unattached notes,
forming no music at all.

The meaning flows
from your guts to mine.
Take in rope. Let some out.
Take it in again!
Anxiety, exquisite care,
trust, doubt and confidence,
sing back and forth
until your head rises
over the lip.

Fifty meters of our umbilicus
pile joyfully at my feet,
released of its duty
to telegraph the poetry
of the climb.

Sitting On Ice

If my elders are any model
this will be an increasing occurrence
over the next years of my life.

Waiting for a call back from a doc
half my age, who has a plan
for my health care
that may or may not include me.

He's smart, no doubt very good at his job,
but he hasn't taken the time to know me.
He doesn't know that I climb mountains,
love the taste of a cold beer in the evening,
write poetry to make sense of life,
struggle with being honest when something's bugging me.

So I sit here wondering how
to let him know that I'm human
and healthy and intend to take charge
of my own health.

Then . . . bowed to the pain,
humbled and calling for help.
Even willing to take the damn drugs
if I can see to the other side
where the mountain ridge still beckons
in the sun.

The Best Therapy I Know

When market share and web presence,
"relationships" on Facebook,
and virtual meetings
confound me,

and my list of things to do includes
joining another networking group,
and attending a webinar
on how to maximize
my search engine exposure,

especially when I discover
that the first thing
I do in the morning
and last at night
is check e-mail,

I go out to bless my wood pile
waiting patiently beside the driveway,
rounds of ponderosa and doug fir,
cut up in the mountains this summer
and stacked through a dry autumn.
Cracked across their map of growth rings,
a history of the past sixty years.

My block, a big old stump on end.
Is it cottonwood?
Countless whacks obscure its story,
now a velvet seat on which
my real work unfolds.

The maul and I—a bit loose in the head,
don't need to be too sharp for splitting,
handle polished, loved, rubbed with oil—
go out to sweat a bit
to earn our winter's warmth.

A study of the round declares where best to aim;
here is where thought, action and results conspire.
Eye fixed on a check to the center,
feet spread and square, far enough back
to avoid a glancing blow.
The maul comes around in back,
hands slide down the piston, up and around,
kundalini flows from the earth,
electric jolt up through legs,
back, shoulders and arms,
flowing down through handle, axe
and into the waiting wood.
CRACK, SPLIT! Pieces fly,
another crease in the stump.
Each round opens in its own character,
its own perfume, a curve around a knot,
a weakness here avoids a cross grain there.

Half an hour of this and I'm sweating,
singing a song through arms
happy to be building January's insurance policy.

Back inside frustrations gone,
hands vibrating at the keys.
How much of this can I bring to my
next virtual meeting?

Thumbing

October '71, five bucks in my pocket.
Bud Hillman, hauling hay
Bozeman to Butte.
Worked for a week,
sixty tons loaded, then unloaded.
Paid a dollar a ton,
plus the best dog I ever knew.
He could climb a tree for a stick.

Hooked up with tree planters
headed to Washington
to plant in the rain.
Slippery slash of Weyerhaeuser Company.

Took a knife from a meat head
waving it around in a bar.
Time to call it a night.

What happened to the guy
with his thumb out on the highway?
Got comfortable, got a mortgage,
a file in a doctor's office.
Quit picking up hitchhikers long ago.

Young men sharpen their edges.
Old guys write poetry and sleep in beds,
calculate risk, soft and dull.

Spineless Adam be damned!
I'm not done living this life.

A Radical Thing

Coming down one of my favorite hikes today
I did a radical thing.
I left the trail for untracked woods.

Took off to make my footprints in soft earth,
to find pine duff ten inches deep,
welcoming my step where none had trod before.
This is not "cutting the trail"
contributing to erosion,
thumbing my nose
at those who spend weekends
lovingly building water bars.
This is a tramping through
deep woods and wild, careful not to step
on cactus, piñon seedling, late Fall flowers.
This is turning the cell phone off
to grab two hours of the sound of wind in the pines.

But what?!
Down in a clearing, a tent,
a pack outside neatly tucked with tarp.
No one home.
In respect, I cruise on past
but can hardly find a trail.
This is not the camp of Homeless Joe.
No trash, no fire pit,
some pains taken
to fit the landscape.

Who then?
A modern-day Thoreau
accomplishing more than turn off his phone.
He's taken care to live here
in the song of the pines,
off the trail,
a radical thing.

Down

It's happened again.
This struggle for meaning and relevance.
Plunking keys in an office
where sunlight has never peeked.
The darkness seeps in.
The slump when back from the wilds.

My inability, over the years
to navigate this descent,
returning to calendars,
numbers and hands on the clock,
has not contributed to my
retirement account.

The wilds, where every action
has direct impact on wellbeing:
Bring enough water to stay hydrated.
Dig fleece out of the pack
when wind kicks up on the summit.
Keep an eye on the clouds.
Tighten shoes to protect toes
on the downclimb.
Denial courts disaster.

Taking care opens to where
blue skies cut like sapphire,
where I've huffed all morning
till there's no more rock above,
yet the air, the birds,
everything yearns for up.
Every breath, every move
connected to vitality,
life on earth seeking the heavens.
What more can I ask?
And how can I bring this light down
to a land of thick conditioned noise?

Tiger Stripes

If we time it right,
Mike and the dogs and I,
we arrive at the top of the trail
as the sun is lowering in the West.

We drink, snack,
remove climbing skins and shorten poles.
The dogs lounge, then romp and roar
as they get ready to go down.

We note the paradox
of putting on clothes
for the descent
while sweating with the exertion
of the climb.
Nylon, head to toe
assuring we will shed the snow.

And down, the first dozen turns
tight in spruce and fir.
Knee deep, adjusting the brakes,
subtle shifts forward and back
watching for sunken snags.
A few whoops escape.

The trudge up hill,
the week's work,
the stress of unsaid things,
starts to melt away.

As evergreen leads into aspen
the sky opens
golden sunlight sheds color
on an almost black and white world.
Tiger stripe shadows
whisper across the snow.

The crystalline blanket rolls down
dipping to every trunk,
rising and falling over Mother Earth's
breasts and stomach.

Like Japanese brush strokes,
it is our art to carve
a delicate line through Her paper.

I fly, ten turns, fifteen!
Panting closer to God.
Too fast,
squeak through a tight spot.

Stop, listen for Mike. Hoot.
He returns it.
I spot his purple snaking toward me.

We breathe in the tiger stripes
remark, as usual,
to bring a camera next time.

Admire our tracks
as the dogs, wallowed and panting
erase the art work.

I'm ready to go,
but he says, "Wait,"
and we stand in the quiet
enjoying the shadow world
we have entered.

The trunks have eyes
winking at us,
scratch marks from a bear
years ago stretching up in the Spring.
They rise up in gold
to meet the New Mexico blue.

I shed another layer of care.
This is what matters.
Dog face covered in snow.

The trunks are bigger, farther apart
my skis get itchy for the dance.
Flying again, sink, rise, swoop,
a clearing, a gate left and right.
His purple off to my left.

High voiced, like a boy, or an elf
my scream echoes in the cathedral.

There are no tracks here before us.
Today this is our sanctuary, our prayer,
the living canvas upon which
we write our joy.
Anyone coming after
will read it perfectly.

One more stop as the sound
of the road below creeps in.
The dogs, now glistening clean,
and happy too for their dance,
catch up.

The tiger skin flattens out
sun sinking fast.
Signs of other skiers,
other artists.

Our peace today seems all too short,
yet what does the clock mean
in this other world.

The light in his eyes,
ease in my shoulders,
and fire in my knees
tell it all.

A Swim

The signs all said private,
no trespassing, danger.

And not being from there
he imagined cottonmouths,
crocodiles and blood suckers.

After he'd been for a swim
in the soft and silky water
inhabiting the color green
from her majesty cypress towering above
with her own murky experiments,

he went up to ask William
—not about the too blue swimming pool—
but the creek.
"We don't recommend it."
he replied.
Then after warning him
about everything but crocs,
proceeded to praise
the living, breathing, flowing stream.

Caught Napping

It was my intent to burn up the trail,
but I've been hijacked by bearberries.
Gushing, red sticky fingers, tart to mouth.
They'll never make it back to town.

Then Shanghai'd by mushrooms,
I hope to wake up
with a glorious hangover
far out in a sea of aspen, spruce and fir.

"When I Met My Muse"
        Thanks to William Stafford

She shook me up and down
rattled my bones,
stood me on my top,
flipped my boat
and bonked my sweetheart on the head.
Nearly drowned us both.
Informed my cocky boatman
he was no longer in charge!

So the banker goes broke,
mechanic's car breaks down,
hail whips the farmer's tomatoes to pulp.

Around every corner She waits
to see if I'll listen this time,
if I'll learn Her song and
sing it truly to my tribe.

She's the one calling me to the road,
to cast off safety lines
and go out to meet people.
The scary ones
who drive pick-ups
with gun racks,
faded paint Mercurys
smelling of old beer,
Indians on their way home,
cowboys just going down the road.

She's here,
offering no insurance or IRA,
but painting my life in blood reds,
sky blues, icy whites and spring green.

She'd rather I dig potatoes out back
than buy them at the store.
And when I decided to kill the pig,
she made him scream
so I couldn't brush it off.

She's fierce and beautiful
and demanding and shy
and she sings
the most compelling song.

The Wild Animal of My Soul

Sometimes a quiet fawn,
or a bright-feathered friend,
timid and shy,
reluctant to poke Her
head out of the deep forest.

Easy to overlook
where She seeks refuge
from my honking traffic
and seeker missiles.

Yet I've glimpsed dark
claw marks on the tree
and overturned logs.
Heard crashings in the bush.

In a gleaming dream,
frightened, legs light,
guts emptied,
I am chased
by a ten-foot moose-bear-elephant,
trunk in the air
roaring his outrage.

Overtaken, entered and filled.
There is no doubt about who is boss.

PEOPLE POLITIC

The Week Before Christmas 2004

Needing a digger,
a human backhoe,
I pull up to Guadalupe corner
and a dozen brown-skinned,
healthy men converge.
I can't open the window fast enough.

How long? *Quatro horas*.
How much? *Diez por hora*.
Cash is understood
outside the immigration laws.

Martin climbs in,
big smile, silver teeth.
Quanto años, Martin? *Diez y ocho*.
He's just a kid.
And we go to work,
quatro pieds, four feet down
to a broken sewer line
clogged with roots.

My Spanish lesson progresses
more than his *Ingles*.
I am the *Jefe*, after all.

He's been here a month,
oldest of five, staying with primo
from Chiapas, where
even their roofs are made of *cemento*.

And I'll bet I'm the first el Norte
to have gotten down in the ditch with him,
swung the pick, slopped in the mud
shoved cold hands in pockets.

Finding *el tubo*, soggy and smelly
we go to the plumbing store for parts.

I get what I need, but he hangs back,
drawn by a roll of copper wire
so old the shopkeeper can't find a price,
can't be bothered,
and feigns ignorance of his mother tongue.
One of us doesn't belong here.

Deciding not to squirm, we stumble
through interpretations,
complete our business and escape.
What can he possibly want one hundred feet
of thin copper wire for?
Back in the truck
I take a guess.
Tu es un artesano?
Si!

We finish our work.
Fill the ditch as cold and dark sink in.
Comes time to pay him
and I recognize a fear I've seen before.
He's been stiffed for his time,
an old story for men without a place.

Then reluctant to let him go,
I offer a ride home.
Feliz Navidad.

Next day I review our lesson,
form a few sentences
remember his wire,
our brotherhood of the ditch.

December 23rd
I buy an English primer,
he's not home when I stop
so I leave it with his cousin's wife.

Christmas day my house is full of white folks,
carols, wine, a ham perhaps, our abundance,
education, belonging and celebration,
not quite taken for granted.

When a guest comes with a funny look,
"There's this guy at the door."
I go. It's Martin.
He won't come in, of course,
brave enough to have come this far,
But offers me an elegant wine glass
woven of wire, a toast full of soul.
His silver smile lights my day.

Sympathy for the Devil

We're obviously in collusion,
have been since Eve's apple.

How could we do without
his deals with the Russians,
his genius at being so bad
we're fooled into not looking
            within.

Too easy to wish for his towers to crumble
while we let our streams run dry.

Does he have designs on our souls,
or is he just keeping his commitment?

We shook hands after all,
traded the garden for awareness,
peach trees for portfolios.
Now we're the ones wanting to renege.

Ali

My neighbor grew up an Afghan prince.
The Russians broke all his fingers,
did unspeakable other things.

Now he smiles, makes jewelry,
brings us jars of apricot preserves,
wears a scarf as if it belongs there.

His bumper sticker reads,
"My religion is lovingkindness."

Un Apologia del Mundo

We got carried away.
It doesn't mean
we're bad people,
that we've all become Nazis.
We continue to be
a big-hearted people,
generous, welcoming, kind.
We got swept into a story.
You understand.
We got scared.
Hoodwinked too,
into believing there was not enough,
and we were powerless.
We forgot about
our "purple mountains majesty"
and "amber waves of grain."
You understand.
Our power lies in remembering
that we "crown our good
with brotherhood
from sea to shining sea."

A Teacher's Plea

under the bridge where you slept last night
and in the drama of the cop chasing you down the street
we are calling you

in the middle of the first rush on Friday night
and the darkness later as it fades to desperation

as you sit to study
unfamiliar as it feels
and you want to get up and scream
how did this happen to me?
we are calling

we are calling you as we struggle
to find the right way to say
you can't show up here blasted
and expect to learn anything
or be safe or help anyone else

and what to do when we suspect
one of you is dealing
or coming just because
you've got nothing better to do

we are calling because
when we were your age
somebody called and it took us forever to answer
and we got hurt and hurt others in the process
and we're hoping whatever kind of love
we can express might make a difference

sometimes you tell us your story
we sit and fumble through trying to listen

a different song drifts through
and we all slow down long enough to savor it

we are calling as if you were our kids
but you're not and it's different
cleaner or maybe we're wiser now
or practicing for when we have some
who knows but we're calling you
not even sure what we have to offer

we are calling to save ourselves
to save our homes from being broken into
to help the nephew who lives in Tennessee
and we haven't seen in years

knowing that our culture has gone terribly wrong
that you may have given up trying to negotiate it

and the only thing that makes sense to us
is to keep on calling

Easter Immigrant

My friend refused to file income taxes this year
afraid he might be identified and deported.

I ran into him and his sister at a gas station Good Friday noontime.
They'd just returned from a six-hour pilgrimage
to the *Santuario de Chimayo*,
a prayer New Mexicans have been walking for generations,
before our borders needed to be defended from aliens.

His palm when I grip it is strong and calloused
by years on a shovel, hammer, horse brush.
He came here with young children
to escape gangs and murder in his country,
to help them build a future in this strange land.

He once won $7000 in a casino
and immediately bought a trailer
so his family could claim roots.

I hired him to help build my house one year.
Never a whisper that it was a palace compared to his.
He helped me butcher the pig to roast,
nodded when I invited him to the celebration,
but didn't attend.
Ashamed, I imagine, of his language,
his work jeans, his culture.
How do I tell him he owns a seat at my table?

And how do I communicate any of this
to the people who would build a wall,
afraid of this big-hearted man
with a light shining out of his chest?

What If?

What if peace was
not talking behind someone's back
even though you wanted to
because they were such a jerk?

What if peace was
making eye contact
with the woman in a hijab
in the grocery store?

Or the vacant kid
hiding under his hoodie
holding a sign, "Help?"

What if peace was
going across the street
to chat with a neighbor
who loved your dog?

What if peace was
feeding the birds
because you like
the way they flit outside the window
as you work?

What if peace was
recycling the tuna can
even though it made the bin smell?

What if peace was
dancing with your mouth open
cause you had to suck in more air
so you could express the joy?

What if peace was
singing for an old man
who could barely respond

because his life had collapsed
and watching his foot begin to tap?

What if peace was
learning how to finally
be quiet inside?

What if peace was
writing a letter to the president
even though you suspect
it will get your name on
his blacklist?

What if peace was
eating more lettuce and broccoli?

What if peace was
just so simple?

REFLECTIONS

A Message

Are only the mystics allowed
to have mystical experiences?
Or is it something the rest of us can do?

On our hike today coming down the ridge
populated with piñon, and an occasional pondo,
I don't remember if it was before or after
Raven stopped us, and we looked up
in awe of the view higher up
of snowfields reaching into the clouds,
that David spoke about Miranda's death
and her message to follow the light.
I glimpsed it, just a flash.
It could have been missed.
In a breath here and gone
beckoning, "Its simple, Jeff,
put out your hand."

Did Jesus do more?
It must have come and gone for him
as he sorted through
all the expectations of others,
his fear of power, of his painful end,
doubt that he should have been a carpenter instead,
and found the courage to reach.

Ever

A single log just won't burn,
but give him a neighbor
and they both blaze on.

My bed is cold
without you.
Yet who can sleep
with a deer?
She bolts at the twitch of an eyebrow
leaving me in a hump
at the base of this aspen
wondering
if she'll ever return.

The Miracle of Now

Consider your next drive to Albuquerque,
Seventy miles, plus or minus, in about an hour.
In the air-conditioned comfort of your auto,
with surround sound from your favorite guru.

And contrast it with a similar journey
just a hundred years ago, in a Model T
if you were rich,
all day in the dust and bumps and cold.

And just because we can explain
how the gasoline passes the valves
and explodes in the cylinders,
how the bearings carry the wheels,
and slide on a film of oil
that once lived in the ground,

it doesn't have to spell commonplace
to the miracle of living right now.

Broken Glass

A boy considers attention
poised between asking
and manipulating for it.

A favorite marble
in his small hand,

dropped on the hard floor,
shatters in one thousand pieces —
stars expanding in the universe.

Each one a light in pitch darkness,
a choice, a direction, an opportunity
to grasp life, and fly out with it,
or to stay and mourn
broken glass.

Can I Stop?

Can I stop the traffic on my road?
Curl up and sleep in the back of the truck,
fitful with the sound of others
driving through the night.
Must I get up,
to join the flow, the hustle,
stiff-necked, unshaved,
mouthful of old tires?
Back on the road
only smoky dreams
of birds and beaver,
forest and streams
remain.

Dad's '49 Flatbed

Stake-sided truck
parked outside the old lilacs
on Payne Avenue.
The men were loading brush
from around the neighborhood.
Suzie and I in the cab
pretending to drive,
rumbling our lips,
pushing chrome buttons.
I probably knew better
and pushed the starter anyway.
Truck lurched.
Men yelled.
Dad furious.
Scared.
Furious.
I didn't want to drive
when I turned sixteen.

Claiming My Name

Middle and Last a family legacy.
Given — I'd like to think —
for one of their admired friends,
a character in a heroic story,
certainly not a politician or movie star.

When old enough to know,
my brother's friends clubbed me with it.
And there was no mistake
When Mom labeled every syllable with "wrong."

Now that I've had time to hear it
shouted across a courtyard
to see if I could go skiing tomorrow.
Whispered in invitation
to come back to bed on Saturday morning.
Spoken into a mic as introduction
to say something worthy.
Over the phone by a dying friend.

But especially now that I've looked in the mirror
to find the sort of guy I'd nod to in a grocery store.
A guy who keeps his phone in his pocket,
where it belongs while in public.
Who's on his way somewhere green and blue,
yet not so fast he can't inquire, then listen.
A guy whose belly hangs over his belt
just enough to prove his appetite,
with plenty of crags carved in his face,
and can find a twinkle on a rainy day.

I think my name belongs to that guy.

Strangers?

New in town,
have to ask directions,
read the signs
and the people.
Do I stick out
like the honky
I imagine they see?
Found my way to DART.
Try not to look too white
as I pay for two hours
on a train full of brown people,
with an unashamed
white woman's voice announcing
"Next stop, Market Station."
As the doors close
a wild dark man
staggers - no, lurches -
his hand into the rubber stop
willing it, through his haze,
to open again.
I don't want him on
my train.
But he manages it,
hands and knees,
crashing side to side,
almost in my lap,
little sky rockets
in his hair.
I see him now
in back of me,
his reflection in the plastic
divider up front.
I'm careful not to turn.
Now here at the door again,
somewhat composed
he manages to get off.
Relieved.

I find the generosity to imagine
he was someone more
than that,
disabled, alert,
despite appearances.
Now, in imagined safety,
I see my reflection
in the same divider,
hat crooked
head wobbling
with the lurch of the train.
Two young women in back
seem to take no notice.
They belong here.

Life At Four Miles An Hour

I can walk four miles an hour,
which is slower than my bicycle,
and notice the sunflowers blooming
with bees busy pollinating.

I can carry on a conversation
at four miles an hour,
and have time to go back to
a point brought up yesterday.

I can listen to you with no
fear for my own gain.

I can sort through my projections of you
to find who you are
at four miles an hour.

We travel four miles an hour
on the river,
and day after day we collect
the landscape
into ourselves
so that it supports us,

like the dried rose on my dashboard
reminding me of your love.

Faster is not better,
for I get ahead of my soul
and then who will notice
the sunflowers,
or take time to float the rivers,

or stop by the side of the road
to write this poem
and weep.

Resolution Bay

I speak to you in curdled milk.
        You answer in veiled honey.
I speak to you kneeling with sponge
in hand to clean the mess from the deck.
        You stand back, hands on hips,
        tight-mouthed, watching.

Lizard screams out, red-eyed.
        You flip the bird and walk.

        Again.

You look at me with a question
from behind your armor.
        My knife is suddenly heavy and dull
        in my hand.
        Heavy and Dull.

You offer a grape from your bag.
        I wonder what wine could come from this?
        Then look at my knife.

        Again.

I speak to you of the breeze
coming in on the tide
and my small son's limp.

You answer in fish
and come back with a crutch.

Tilt

I am sorry. I'm so sorry
that the kid I passed on the way out here
to my forest:
    the kid on tilt in the back of the bus
    crossing from Llano St. to Saint Mike's,
    all wrapped and harnessed
    so he wouldn't bounce,
    yet they couldn't capture his tongue,
    his willow-wand eyes,
    his mind
    who knows where. . .
so that I'm certain he will never
sit on this piece of warm earth
in this bear-scratched and golden
aspen grove far above
the sound of traffic.

Yet I wonder if somewhere
in the wandering bus of his soul
he too weeps
for the life of his world.

Aging's Paradox

My mirror belies seventy winters.
Nor does my spirit shrink
from celebrating work and play.

Spending an hour in the ditch
with pick and shovel however
—no stranger in the past—
prompts a visit to the doctor.

And despite ligaments coming undone,
my loved one's urgence to slow down rankles.

For these five-fingered hands singing
through shoulder and back
arc up and around with all
the youthful power of the earth,
be it pick or maul or hewed spear.

And these breathing, bleeding, tree trunks of legs
love nothing more than pumping up the mountain
in anticipation of flying our way down.

I hope to end my days inhabiting my miracle,
singing, flying, crying, chasing joy,
so eager to drink this earthy life.

Yet it's not so simple.
With seventy winters
comes a certain appreciation
for naps and baths,
going off on a wander
instead of an expedition.

And my drive to speed,
cutting it close,
finding that old edge,
may be nothing more than

denial of the fact.

Which calls the old warrior
to examine himself more truthfully.

I've heard myself say,
You know, my knees
have been good to me
all these years.
I think I'll skip this run
and sip hot chocolate in the cabin.

As long as you don't
expect me to stay home
on the next powder day.
Or abandon this elegant ditch
we've taken such care
and pride to carve.

Grief

Tide comes in again,
from the center of the Earth
a burst of nerves in solar plexus,
rising in salty waves
up behind my eyes.

Your absence leaves me
rootless
and afraid,
old friend.
Not wanting to come home
to the ground from which you sprung.
Where entering the gate
all I meet is me.

Tides are pulled by the moon
queen of the night.
Owner of my loneliness.

Kodi's End

I've just finished digging a grave
for my best friend.
Four worms killed,
casualties of my fervor
to participate in ending his life.

He has lurched himself into the house
avoiding a light rain just started.
The day, dawning clear, has steadily grown dark.

Since I've made the bizarre decision,
I'm ready to go.
Yet the vet hasn't called back.
Impatient.

Whose life is this anyway?
And how did I come to take responsibility
for its end?

Like the drops beading on lilac leaves,
I have drunk of his vitality.
My anchor through the dissolution of a marriage,
nearly losing my boy,
too many girlfriends come and gone.

He has kept my feet on the ground
rejoicing more than a few mountain tops.

I fear that my boat will drift now.
Yet holding on won't work.
His time has come.

And we agreed at the beginning
that I would be in charge.

Proof of God?

If it weren't enough to have Lilies,
their purple tongues
lapping up Spring rains,
or September Marigolds
the envy of every Tudor ruff,
then surely majestic Ponderosa
standing in glory on his hill,
softest carpet of burnt orange needles
spread at his feet.

But we have to consider
the sense to love all that,
bare feet caressed as we
approach his piney majesty
pulled in by the vanilla butterscotch
deep in every crevice of his bark.

Why would we have developed
such appreciation?
To swoon in drunken rapture?
My faithful hound expresses it
in her romp after rabbit,
but knows it not.
She cuts through Lilies
as if they were common grass.
Surely something hungry
and grand built this body,
a living vessel for wonder.

Ode to Jake Sully*

Dirt and grass and cottonwood leaves
—despite my fear of broken glass—
welcome my toes so much more
than gravel or pavement
or the inside of my shoes.

*main character in the movie Avatar

Self

I have been blessed with a body that works.
No, more than works. It loves to work.
I can barely identify the subtle shifts,
knees, hips to back, wings stretched then tucked,
necessary to carve a turn at high speed
through snow changing from cloud
to day-old mashed potatoes.
And so often I end up face down in the stuff
exhaling a mouthful before coming up to laugh
in celebration of electric pulses
seemingly on their own within me.

Or stopping for water to find hours gone by
while mixing and pouring cement
on a crispy sky-blue November day.
The rhythmic back and forth of hoe.
Shoulders feeling, not seeing, a perfect texture.
Then the scrape of trowel, back and forth
wrist and forearm describing the orbit of the moon,
seeking satin in the alchemy of mud
transforming to marble.

Our ancestors ran with bison
learned to flow out of body into the herd
until the right animal revealed himself.

We sit at desks exercising our fingers to our peril.

Get out, visit your garden, grow a blister
between thumb and finger.
Climb a tree higher than safe.
Dive into living water, brown or green,
come up spitting, whooping,
full of your Self!

Amy

My stepdaughter sent me a card for Father's Day.
We've been distant since she married . . .
But this card shows a wide-eyed toddler
not quite laughing, gripping her dad's toes
as she rides his feet in an "airplane"
high above the living room floor.

I remember pushing—her mom protecting—
her to reach out, higher, arch!
Can't imagine the dance she had to learn
to negotiate our turns.

And now, she's running marathons.
I'll bet I could still hold her up.

Caroline

"Have you got a minute?"
was our code for:
"Can I have a hug?"
"Do you still love me?"
And she did.
Every time.

I thought of her as the Queen of New York.
High-powered PR executive, limos, celebrities,
picture in the paper.

But she came home to her brother's house
in the suburbs for holidays.
Rolled up her sleeves
and did a poor job of stirring the gravy
(according to Mom).

I was busy and loud, fast and underfoot.
Her husband decided:
"Children should be neither seen nor heard."
She countered:
"Have you got a minute?"

I came home from college.
She'd retired. We sat.
She'd seen HAIR!
Wanted to know about drugs,
got upset when I told her I'd seen God,
afraid she might miss something.

Later, all hooked up and dying,
I asked how she was with God.
"I'm at peace with my maker,
I'm just not ready to leave this adventure."

It's been thirty years and I've right now
"got a minute."

Ripley

What does one do with a place
that gets under your skin
in a world calling itself "real estate"
and all we do is hop in the car
to go somewhere else?

How to manage the ache
when you haven't been there for years
and an old friend sends a picture
that breaks your heart?

Knowing part of your soul
resides on that scrappy green point
where the tide rushes in and out
day after day, filling then emptying the bay.
Where seagulls shit on the big rock
and fog rolls in from the ocean
making everything moist and soft.
Where just the memory of the smell of balsam
on the winding path
takes you straight to heaven.

When the marketing coach says
poetry doesn't belong in your new website
if you want to appeal to corporate.

But you know corporate is made up of people
who know places like this,
that anchor our lives, hold us together,
and should we forget,
we'll surely be lost.

Wounds

Nobody escapes this life without wounds.
Most of us deny them
living in favor of
our imaginations.

Some are willing
to look at them
in pain.

Yet we get lost
in the ecstasy of
the agony,
always searching
for the band-aid.

A few are able to live
reasonable lives
in spite of them,
dancing between
the dirty dishes and dessert.

And only a handful
learn to celebrate them.

We call those mad.

Alone?

All your life
you've been complaining
about being alone.
But now,
you come back,
by choice.

Who is it
sitting with you?

The one with tanned hands,
strong shoulders,
nimble feet.

Yes, he's the one.

You met on the peak today.
Then coming down in the rain,
a zigzag path
through wet flowers,

dirty strawberries
so sweet
on his tongue.

What If Forgiveness?

What if my forgiveness of you
were the key to my salvation?

What if I could answer the call
from the girlfriend who stiffed me
fifteen years ago,

or the buddy who slept with my partner
back in the seventies,

or my mom, ten years dead, who,
even after she'd blown her head up in a stroke,
couldn't resist comparing my brother and me,
and no matter who came out on top,
drove a knife into each of our souls.

What if the call was her next-to-last breath
and she wanted to be forgiven?

What if she didn't even know what she was
asking for and had the same bullshit going,
and died and I didn't answer because I was still pissed?

What if I could put away my bile
and answer as if she loved us both all along,
in her broken way, in her terribly wounded way,
in the only way she could?

52904178R00068

Made in the USA
Lexington, KY
23 September 2019